Smithsonian kids

Reptiles

Brenda Scott Royce

PRE-LEVEL 1: ASPIRING READERS

 LEVEL 1: EARLY READERS

 LEVEL 2: DEVELOPING READERS

- Simple factual texts with mostly familiar themes and content
- Concepts in text are supported by images
- Includes glossary to reinforce reading comprehension
- Repetition of basic sentence structure with variation of placement of subjects, verbs, and adjectives
- Introduction to new phonic structures
- Integration of contractions, possessives, compound sentences, and some three-syllable words
- Mostly easy vocabulary familiar to kindergartners and first-graders

 LEVEL 3: ENGAGED READERS

 LEVEL 4: FLUENT READERS

Silver Dolphin Books
An imprint of Printers Row Publishing Group
A division of Readerlink Distribution Services, LLC
9717 Pacific Heights Blvd, San Diego, CA 92121
www.silverdolphinbooks.com

ISBN: 978-1-68412-474-9
Manufactured, printed, and assembled in Rawang, Selangor, Malaysia.
Second printing, June 2021. THP/06/21
25 24 23 22 21   2 3 4 5 6

Reviewed by Jeremy Jacobs, Research Collaborator, Department of Vertebrate Zoology, National Museum of Natural History, Smithsonian.

For Smithsonian Enterprises:
Kealy Gordon, Product Development Manager
Jill Corcoran, Director, Licensed Publishing
Janet Archer, DMM, Ecom and D-to-C
Carol LeBlanc, President

Image Credits: Thinkstock, Getty Images

What Is a Reptile?

Snakes, turtles, lizards, and alligators are all types of reptiles.
They have dry skin covered in scales or bony plates.
There are more than eight thousand types of reptiles in the world.

Really Cool Reptiles

The Galapagos tortoise is the world's largest tortoise.
This giant tortoise weighs more than a full-grown gorilla!
It can live to be over one hundred years old.

The male Jackson's chameleon has three horns on its head.
It can move its eyes independently of each other.

The blue-tongued skink is named for the color of its tongue.

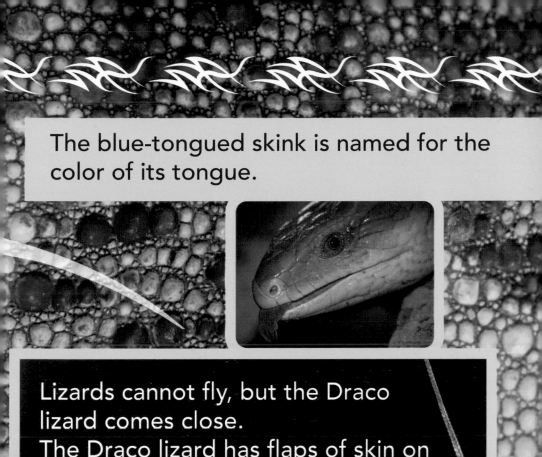

Lizards cannot fly, but the Draco lizard comes close.
The Draco lizard has flaps of skin on both sides of its body.
It spreads these flaps and glides in the wind!
Draco lizards can soar one hundred feet in the air.

Reptile Homes

Reptiles live all over the world, except Antarctica.
A reptile's home is called its **habitat**.
Different reptiles live in different types of habitats.

Some reptiles live in the desert.

Others live in the trees of rainforests.

Reptiles can also live in lakes, rivers, and oceans.
Reptiles like to bask in the sun to get warm.
They find shade to cool off.

What's for Dinner?

Different reptiles eat different foods.
Small reptiles eat insects.
A chameleon catches a cricket with its long, sticky tongue.

Desert tortoises eat grass, plants, and flowers.
The Komodo dragon is a large lizard that can eat an entire deer!

Snakes are **carnivores**.
They eat other animals for food.
Snakes' favorite foods are mice,
birds, eggs, and frogs.
Snakes don't use teeth
to chew their food.
Instead, they swallow
it whole.

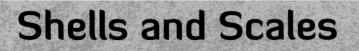

Reptiles may be smooth, rough, or bumpy. Reptiles are not slimy!

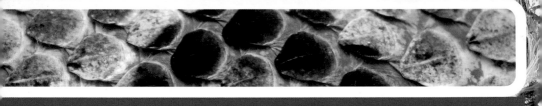

Snake scales come in different shapes and colors.
Scales overlap like tiles on the roof of a house.

Reptiles replace their skin as they grow.
A snake sheds its skin all at once.
Special scales on the underside of snakes give
them traction so they can move.

Most turtles and all tortoises have hard shells.
The star tortoise has star-shaped markings
on its shell.

Reptiles don't have fur or feathers.
So how do they keep warm?
Reptiles are cold-blooded.
Cold-blooded means they cannot
control their body heat.

Reptiles' body heat depends on their **environment**. Reptiles need heat from the sun to keep warm.

They rest on a rock in a sunny area. When it is too cold, reptiles become inactive.

They don't have sweat glands, so they can't cool off when it's hot. They have to move to a shady spot to cool off.

Hide and Seek

Some reptiles have great **camouflage**. Their colors and patterns blend in with rocks, branches, or trees.
Camouflage helps reptiles stay safe. They can easily hide from **predators**.
A leaf gecko looks like it's part of a plant.

Chameleons can change color to match their surroundings.

The Gaboon **viper** is a large snake that lives in the forest.
The patterns on the viper's back help it blend in with leaves on the forest floor.

Some snakes have special coloring that is a warning to predators. The coral snake has pretty colors. But watch out! This snake has a dangerous bite. The coral snake's bright colors warn others to stay away.

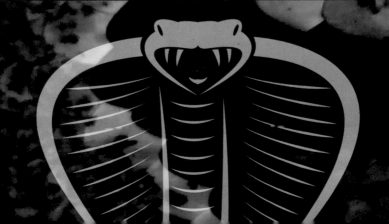

A rattle is this snake's alarm. It is made of a material called keratin. Human fingernails are made of keratin too. A rattlesnake shakes the rattle at the end of its tail. The sound tells others "Beware!"

A cobra can spread out its neck to make it look bigger.

Turtles and Tortoises

What's the difference between a turtle and a tortoise?

turtle

Turtles live near water. Sea turtles live in the ocean. Other turtles live in freshwater such as ponds or lakes. Their webbed feet help them swim.

tortoise

Tortoises live on land and they do not have webbed feet.

Both turtles and tortoises have shells for protection.
Some turtles can suck their head and legs inside their shell for safety!

Turtles and tortoises don't have teeth.
They bite their food with a sharp upper beak.

Snakes eat other animals for food.
Some snakes kill their **prey** by
squeezing it.
Boas and pythons are squeezers.
They are called constrictors.

Other snakes kill their prey by biting it.
Rattlesnakes are biters.
Rattlesnakes have sharp teeth called **fangs**.
A rattlesnake uses its fangs to inject **venom** into its prey.
The venom can kill the prey.
Some snakes have stronger venom than other snakes.

Lizards

There are more than four thousand types of lizards.
Iguanas, chameleons, and geckos are all lizards.
A green iguana can be six feet long!
The green iguana lives in the tropical rainforest.

The gecko's toes are great at gripping!
The gecko's special toes help it climb up walls.

This colorful creature is a collared lizard.
The black stripes around its neck look like a shirt collar.
They are one of just a few lizards that can run using only their back legs.

Dragons!

These are not fairy-tale dragons.
They cannot fly.
They don't breathe fire.

These dragons belong to the lizard family.
The Komodo dragon is the world's largest
lizard. It can be
ten feet long
and weigh three
hundred pounds!

The bearded dragon has spiky scales on its throat.
The bearded dragon inflates its "beard" like a balloon.

Chinese water dragons love to swim.
They can even eat underwater!
Chinese water dragons can stay submerged underwater for almost thirty minutes.

Alligators and Crocodiles

What's the difference?

alligator

crocodile

Alligators have short, wide heads in the shape of a U. Crocodiles have heads that are long and pointed like the letter V. Both alligators and crocodiles spend most of their time in water.

Both alligators and crocodiles have strong senses, which make them excellent hunters. Their senses are more powerful than those of most other reptiles.

The gharial is a crocodile with a long, skinny snout.
The gharial has more than one hundred teeth in its mouth.

The saltwater crocodile is the world's biggest reptile.
It can grow to be seventeen feet long!

Baby Reptiles

Sea turtle mothers bury their eggs on the beach.
When the eggs hatch, the baby turtles race to the sea.
A sea turtle may lay one hundred eggs at one time.
That's a lot of brothers and sisters!

Crocodile moms protect their babies.
A crocodile mother carries her babies in her mouth to keep them safe.
Sometimes, the babies ride on her back.

Baby rattlesnakes are more dangerous than adults because they can't control their venom.
Reptiles can be big, small, colorful, or fierce. Reptiles are amazing creatures!

Reptiles **QUIZ**

1. Which is NOT a reptile?
   a) Snake
   b) Frog
   c) Turtle

2. What do chameleons use to catch their food?
   a) Tail
   b) Claws
   c) Tongue

3. How do reptiles keep warm?
   a) By wrapping their bodies in leaves
   b) By resting in a sunny area
   c) By huddling with other reptiles

4. Which snake squeezes its prey?
   a) Boa
   b) Rattlesnake
   c) Cobra

5. Which reptile has special toes that help it climb up walls?
   a) Chameleon
   b) Gecko
   c) Draco lizard

6. What are snakes that squeeze their prey called?
   a) Rattlesnakes
   b) Vipers
   c) Constrictors

Answers: 1) b 2) c 3) b 4) a 5) b 6) c

GLOSSARY

camouflage: an animal's coloring that helps it hide and blend in

carnivores: animals that eat other animals

environment: the area and conditions that surround an animal

fangs: sharp teeth snakes use to deliver venom

habitat: place where an animal lives

predators: animals that hunt other animals for food

prey: animals that are hunted by other animals for food

venom: poison produced by some snakes

viper: a type of snake that has venom